Barnaby was born in Harpenden, Hertfordshire and has been writing poetry ever since he was 15. He had a good loving upbringing and lived in Harpenden for 22 years when, at the age of 22, he went to Barnsley College to study music creative technology as an HND. He moved to London in 2003 and has been living there ever since.

This book is dedicated to Tizzy. I will always love you.

Barnaby Duffett

BEYOND THE BLUE

AUSTIN MACAULEY PUBLISHERS®

LONDON · CAMBRIDGE · NEW YORK · SHARJAH

A CIP catalogue record for this title is available from the British Library.

ISBN 9781035867639 (Paperback)
ISBN 9781035867646 (ePub e-book)

www.austinmacauley.com

First Published 2025
Austin Macauley Publishers Ltd®
1 Canada Square
Canary Wharf
London
E14 5AA

Now She Rests

Now she rests upon our hearts.
This ending brings another start.
A fruit has fallen from the tree.
Its seed will spread in history.

Another drop into the sea.
To drift in tides so raw and free.
The scales are shed.
The next step is here.
As we remember her presence
Through the years.

Now the sun sets and the midnight
Masquerade is revealed.
There is no time to pause for breath.
As fate has become so definite and sealed.

Into eternity, she gently drifts.
With such dignity as her spirit lifts.
There is only now as the earth shifts.
Don't waste it because she never did.

Chorus of Heaven

She rises to a chorus of heaven in my heart.
I believe that we should never part.
There is space to be found within our lives.
That twist and turn like butterflies.

She lifts me up she makes me calm.
She bathes my head in liquid balm.
I want to make a brand new day.
Another act inside this play.

One day, we will quit this chase.
Another facet of the human race.
The tree that bends the tides that turn.
There is always a chance for us to learn.

A Feast of Light

A feast of colour.
A feast of light.
A taste of nature's pure insight.
I wander now in winter's calm.
There is no rush and no alarm.

I listen to the magic sounds.
The wings that beat.
The bird that grounds.
I am at peace.
I know my place.
Life's drudgery gives way to happiness and grace.

There is a change inside my brain.
This world will never be the same.
The chain has broken.
The cloud has burst.
The smoke has left my head at last.

I know that I can be much stronger than this.
I can dispel this poisoned kiss.
I no longer want to stare into the abyss.
I can charm the snake.
I do not fear its hiss.

She pulls me in with hastening speed.
She is the saviour of all creeds.
She lifts the flag on a new territory.
She is here to tell the final story.

Eternities Wing

Love blooms like the flowers in spring.
My heart beats like the pendulum of time.
Angels dance on eternity's wing.
And the strength in your mind is the perfect rhyme.

Let us dance away the pain and the fear.
Let us not wait for this feeling to die.
I can see the horizon drawing us near.
Take my hand and we can conquer the ever-changing sky.

Do not betray me on this darkest night.
Do not leave me naked in these screaming streets.
Show me the colours beyond black and white.
Help me to break from the executioner's seat.

I would bare my soul for a look in your eyes.
I would draw my blood on the canvas of fate.
It is only a coward that sits back and denies.
What towers we can build beyond the prisons of hate?

Under the Whispering Tree

As we sit under the whispering tree.
That talks of magic and harmony.
Laughter sings in her overladen bow.
A song that most just don't allow.

And as I meander through the clouds.
The time has come to escape these crowds.
Love seeps right through the whispering tree.
And nature's voice will follow me.

But now there is a screeching sound.
As the earth gives way to solid ground.
Trapped fast in the river of material dreams.
Held tight in this catastrophic cathedral it seems.

Let angels cast their spell once more.
In the bellowing landscape tinged by the sun.
Let us not mistake what this world is for.
We have to stand before we can run.

I yearn to see your bewildering kingdom.
Set sail in your treasures again.
To taste the abundant fruits of freedom.
And find solace in your sweet velvet domain.

Broken Feather

Broken feather caught by the wind.
Where did you come from?
Where will your journey end?
How do you make your way in this breathless kingdom?

As faces shuffle like alien prisoners to their offices.
How do you find space to touch my heart?
With such purity for which you make so many sacrifices.
With such love for which you have always fought.

Beware the tide that throws us into the reality where nature
becomes a number.
Colour is just a code.
But you shoulder the weight with care free from slumber.
You never take for granted this paralysing load.

You bring this race begging on its knees.
Your endless grace is the boat to sail these seas.
Broken feather I know that we can mend.
We don't have to be clever.
We don't have to pretend.

A New Story

This world has no end in my lifetime.
The stars will never go out in my lifetime.
The seas will never wash away in my lifetime.
And for now, as we crumble in the uncertain chaos of
billions of years.
Time moves on.

Always changing with every expanding nuance.
Constantly evolving with every turn of the wheel.

And as I look to the heavens once more.
The swirling symmetry of constellations that we give a
uniform shine so clearly.
Suited in their armour.

Love tingles in my minuscule being.
Safe in the knowledge that there is something more.
A new story to be told.
A new chapter to be written.
A new key to the door.

My senses are crystallised by their beauty.
I am but elemental dust.
I am born and I shall die.
There is nothing else but to exist, as we all do.
Trying to get by.
Surviving like packs of wolves in the moonlight.

The World Comes Calling

The world comes calling once more.
The slow sun breaks the silence, and I am lifted to another plane.
The crystal clouds paint pastel pictures of ecstatic joy as we are carried away on chariots of emotion.
This day is the time to make good our lives.

A lubricant of inspiration hits me once more and my senses catch alight in the chaos of the race.
An imprint from the fingers of eternal hope.
No longer needing your advice.
No longer waiting for a slice.
No longer falling to my knees.
For the answer is blowing on the breeze.

The bell that chimes and calls in the day.
Will no longer make me run away.
I open the vent that fuels the fire.
And cast the spell that is desired.
One day, I will hold your hand once more.
And peer through the crack that shines light through the door.

So lift your head up to the sky where we don't have to wonder why.
With imagination, we can spread the wings that lift us out of bed.
Our time will come to swim in the river.
And help our spirit be delivered.

A Fire, It Rages

A fire, it rages into the night.
The clouds, they glow with pure insight.
Our senses burn and we know it's right.
To make this hour a pure delight.

She puts her hand on my shoulder.
I want to be with her until we grow much older.
She sets me straight.
She lifts me up.
She pours her light into my cup.

I yearn for the love she has inside.
Together on this plane, we can glide.
This world is alive and open wide.
From this chance for hope, we cannot hide.

The City Spills Out

The city spills out like the milk of human kindness into the
gentle rolling countryside.
A new beginning has come my way.
A lifeline from the stagnant pool of the meandering day.

She spreads her wings like a golden fire.
She catches life with sweet desire.
No longer will we dwell in the shadowy more.
With imagination, we will fly across the jagged wire.

The Candle

There is a candle that burns inside my brain.
It knows when to flicker and change the plain.
It sometimes burns brightly.
It is sometimes put out.
But there is always a chance to relight it.

This world has the match.
My thoughts undo the latch.
The doors open wide for now.
And the night burns slowly like a smouldering ember
waiting to have life breathed into it once again.

Together we can write a new score.
Together, we can paint a new picture on the totem pole of
time.
Ever ascending to the sky.
We dance as the candle flickers once more.

Throw Away Your Chains

The harmony of the coast breathes new life into my veins.
The gathering storm I try to ignore as I throw away my
chains.

We hunker together for safety.
We walk like lonely sheep.
We hunger for peace and love.
In an ocean that is so deep.

Time to take stock of what we have.
Time to not worry about how we behave.
Don't let the darkness bring you down.
Don't let the bitterness become your slave.

Window of Opportunity

The day comes crashing in through a window of
opportunity.
It seems that walls are closing in on me.
Afraid to be true and so eager for me to lose.
Trying seems like a lost cause.

You penetrate my mind like a jackhammer.
Crushing what I once knew to be real.
I long for the time when we can speak without persecution.
A time when we can escape this retribution.
Without being put down.
Without this impossible expectation.

I just want to hold you once again.
I just want to feel your fingers through my hair.
You take away the pain.
You make me feel sunshine through the rain.
With you, I can find the light that does not restrain.

Nature Is Locked Away

Nature is locked away.
The neon flow of human progression weighs heavily on the soul.
Locked in the café, we scrape and scramble without the key.
Trying to find purpose.
Looking for a reason to live in this decaying society.

You are the reason to live.
We are forgetting what we once knew to be true.
We have forgotten the lesson in this never-ending blue.
We have forgotten what it's like to be human.
What it is to be real.
There is a heart that will always be waiting for you in this ever-changing blue.

Endless Feeling

When will this darkness ever end?
All I ever wanted was a friend.
The night comes in with a cold, twisted vision.
As I yearn to find a new ambition.

The stars, they glint like cosmic troubadours.
And I am lost underneath their glare.
They stare into my soul.
And wash light into this hole.

They take me back.
They bring me down.
They make me miss you in this town.
If only you would open the door.
I love you still with all my heart.
You know we shouldn't be apart.
I want to touch your very being.
With songs that speak with endless feelings.

Walls of Confusion

Walls of confusion surround my brain.
Sheets of delusion fall like the rain.
I don't know how long I can take the strain.
Of a perception that slowly drives me insane.

Your liquid skin is like the sun.
It stops my thoughts on this train that runs.
And shows me what's real and can't be won.

I need to break these walls of confusion.
That locks in my soul and dampens the illusion.
Armies of negativity assault my senses.
And hem me in with barbed wire fences.

If only you could breach these wild defences.
And find a new wavelength of good instances.

Touch Paper of Desire

The misty melon moon lights the touch paper of desire.
The fuse burns like a crematorium fire.
Senses scattered and confused.
Through the palace of wisdom, our souls swim higher.
As the ocean of night laps up against the corners of my mind.
Corroding this imprisoning wire.

It is time to step out.
Time to step across.
As intoxication rings in the changes.
A nonphysical dimension is there to be discovered.
As our imagination rearranges a world that has lost direction.
The express train rattles on.
Through gentle hills and sun-kissed mountains.
There is only one true destination.
The one we all must face.

It Is Inside You

It is within you.
It lies crackling inside you.
You cannot escape it.
You have to face it.
Like embers that are waiting to be blown by the hurricane
that whips inside your head.
The secret desire that comes to you when you sleep like a
dream inside your bed.

The clock is ticking.
The wolf is at the door.
You cannot wait for a solution anymore.
You have to search for the gem that will shine brighter than
the pain.
Things will never be the same again.
No time to be fumbling around in the dark.
You have to forge a brand-new spark.
In a reality that is so bare and stark.
It is time to spread your wings and sour like a Lark.

Butterfly

Deep in the heart of a diesel-fuelled progress.
You flutter by without a care.
Lost in the surge of society's prowess.
You stand for a love that fills the air.

Not thinking of your plight.
Not concerned with what is wrong and right.
You exist like a natural spring of hope.
Then you were gone.
Just like a glint in the eye.
Your wings throbbed with the beat of a better world.
That sings with the promise of a liquid awakening.
Where you climb out from under like infinite imagination.
Nothing will ever die in your essence.
You are nature's beauty.

The Love That Echoes

The love that echoes throughout the years.
The ties that bind and swallow our fears.
Now is the time to throw away restraints.
To build new houses and not pretend we are saints.

The chains tighten in our minds.
They leave us waiting far behind.
Away from intoxication and dilution of our thoughts.
There is a place where in this prison we are not caught.

You make your own demons.
You hide in your pale delusions.
You make a mockery of the world with your negative
conclusions.

Words That Crush

Words can set you free but they can also crush the very
essence of you.
Like lungs, filling with water in a drowning view.
What horrible creatures we can be!
To put each other down externally.

It is only our own problems that we fight against.
Only our own demons that we run from.
Locked up and fenced in.
Why can we not look for the best in people?
Mend the cracks in this crumbling steeple.
We are not all devils weak and feeble.
There is good in everyone.
It doesn't matter where we have gone.
It is where we are that matters.
We must find a new song.

Not one of death and destruction.
We must learn to love ourselves.
And question what it is that lets the dust gather on the
shelves.

The Misty Blue Mountains

The vast array of constellations melts into the misty blue
mountains.
The jewels in the crown of the sleeping village.
The sun burns embers in the background to an ecstatic vista.
Planets swirl and beckon us closer to the night.
As we prepare to let ourselves loose through the gates of
heaven.
A new twist begins in the turning wheel of experience.
The soul is like a burning ember that is never extinguished.
Sometimes it flares with pure light
Burning with unadulterated energy.
We ride out like war horses.
Emotions of fire.
Waiting for the movement to take us higher.

Deliver Us from Hurt

What an uncertain time we live in.
One where all we do is strive to win.
To beat others down and crush them with sin.
There must be more than this hollow shore.
As we sell our souls in gift card stores.
The crack of hopeless crumbling floors.

Told how to think.
Pushed to the brink.
Locked up in cells that divide until there is nothing left to do
but wink.

If only there wasn't such destruction.
If only there was more invention.
The world sleeps now in dreaming slumber.
Maybe one day we will wake up from the war.
Maybe one day we will know what life is for.
Not to kill the milk of Mother Nature.
But to plant new seeds and let them grow.
To throw away the shackles of hate.

Because we have the key.
Only you can set yourself free.
You have to want to make the change.
In a world that sometimes seems so strange.
With love, our hearts can rearrange.

Guilt Edged

You are what you believe you are.
It is in your head.
This guilt passes through you like a serpent.
Ever shifting in the sand.
The sand that meets the sea.
Every grain is a person's impression.
Corroded by the waves.
Forgotten eyes floating in the breeze.
You are no better than a human.
You are no brighter than this lack of reason.
A wave of emotion is passing you by.
This feeling is out of season.
It makes me want to cry.

But in my madness, I am sane.
The sun has come to hold back the rain.
Will you help me make my heart good again?
As pathways form inside my brain.

Universal Drift

We are all unique and equal in the universal drift.
As an individual as a fingerprint.
As precious as a snowflake.
We are woven in an eternal stitch.
Along the stepping-stones, we traverse the river wake.

Who knows what tapestry will be made by our final view?
What creature will wear our comfort?
What family will be born from our knowledge?

More than imagination.
Blown by the wind in all directions.
A link in the chains of evolution.
We are alive with love.
A flag to the sign of new consciousness.
A bridge over the wine of confusion.
We are alive and in love.
Beyond the search for human reason.
We are alive.

Let Flowers Bloom

Let flowers bloom.
Let angels sing.
Let us make some room for a brand-new spring.
Open all the doors and let in the light.
For love, it roars like a fire in the night.

Let us strike the chord that turns a key.
That moves the earth for you and me.
The past is a murmur, a memory.
Let us embrace the future as bright as it can be.

No time for doubt.
No time for pain.
As hand in hand, we can hold back the rain.
Who knows where we can travel on this train?
As happiness explodes inside the brain.

So let rivers flow and burst in streams.
And through the patchwork of time, we can follow their dreams.
In this crumbling world, we can patch up the seems.
And in unity, we will know just what life means.

So let flowers bloom.
Let angels sing.
And a brand new tune in our ears will ring.
With this unbridled energy, our hearts will wing.
And together we can solve anything.

Unlock the Door

Let language speak its marvellous roar.
Let it hold us tight and unlock the door.
For thoughts are fine but have no weight.
If they don't reach out and communicate.
Sometimes I feel I could shout so loud.
Sometimes I want to lose this crowd.
So much to give but no platform to say.
So many prisons that get in the way.

We are together in this blessed race.
But we are the ones that can blemish the face.
In this world of suffering and terminal pain.
Is there anyone who will hold back the rain?
Only you can unlock the door.
Only you can speak life's marvellous roar.

You Hurt Me

You stop me in my tracks.
You draw me out of sync.
You make me out of time.
Until I just can't really think.

You hurt me on the ground.
You toss me in the air.
You make me drink the poison until I really just don't care.

You hurt me with your words.
You kill me in your sleep.
You make me believe the absurd.
Until life is very cheap.

You leave me far behind.
With too much time to think.
You make out to be someone.
Then you wash me down the sink.

The Sea That Never Ends

There is a sea that never ends.
Crashing around my shores.
Pulling me under.
Ripping up my heart.
There is a world that rarely bends.
Coiling around me like a vine.
Alive like a black hole.
Waiting to swallow me.

There is a road I just can't follow.
I am on my knees now.
There is no destination that can help me.
Only you with your bold smile.
For you, I would walk a thousand miles.
Only you can help me.

But the rain tumbles down in my world.
It has been reduced to an infinite point.
Where is the love that once galloped across the world with
such joyous abandon?
What can I do to silence the ghosts that hurl bricks inside my
soul?
Battering down the walls.
Penetrating the barriers.

Is There a Cure?

Now it seems the pain will last forever.
Now it seems there is no cure.
I reach out past these bewildering and strangling thoughts.
There must be someone who can give me peace of mind.
I must not fight it.
I must let it swallow me.
Before, I can be reborn.

People's lives take on momentum.
And mine stands still.
Trussed up in this fortress.
Locked up behind the door.
Freedom fades. Love is strange.
I cannot feel you anymore.

I used to dream a thousand dreams.
Now I just sleep for a million years.
It hits you like a fist of flesh and bone.
No sympathy.
No compassion.
Nothing that lasts.

I want to drink from the eternal stream.
I want to live again.
The wind howls at me once more.
The wolf is baying at my senses.
The key has been turned to lock the door.

Printed in Great Britain
by Amazon

58517249R00030